Bump 2 Baby

A Young Person's Guide to Pregnancy

Paul McCabe

Jessica Kingsley *Publishers*
London and Philadelphia

First published in 2013
by Jessica Kingsley Publishers
116 Pentonville Road
London N1 9JB, UK
and
400 Market Street, Suite 400
Philadelphia, PA 19106, USA

www.jkp.com

Library of Congress Cataloging in Publication Data
McCabe, Paul, 1972–
Bump 2 baby : a young person's guide to pregnancy / Paul McCabe.
pages cm
ISBN 978-1-84905-416-4 (alk. paper)
1. Teenage pregnancy--Health and hygiene--Popular works.
2. Teenage mothers--Health and hygiene--Popular works.
3. Pregnant women--Health and hygiene--Popular works.
I. Title. II. Title: Bump to baby.
RG556.5.M42 2013
618.200835--dc23
2013004881

British Library Cataloguing in Publication Data
A CIP catalogue record for this book is available from the British Library

ISBN 978 1 84905 416 4
eISBN 978 0 85700 776 6

Printed and bound in China

Acknowledgements

A huge thank you to Amy, Kelly, Stacey, Claire, Charlotte, Becki and Janine for their commitment, ideas and enthusiasm in the production of Bump to Baby. Without them this guide would not have been designed, produced and printed.

Acknowledgement and thanks also go to all of those professionals who contributed their time, comments and advice to the guide.

The facilitation support team that worked on the original draft of the book included Christine McCabe, of the Young People's Health Project (Birmingham Youth Service), and Lorraine Williams, Children's Centre Midwife (Tame Valley and Kitts Green – Heart of England NHS Foundation Trust).

The 'Bump 2 Baby' group and their children.

www.thisisplum.co.uk

Always Seek Advice!

Disclaimer: This book is for guidance only. Whilst we strive to make it as accurate as possible, neither the author, publishers nor the associated agencies or people involved in this project accept any liability or responsibility whatsoever for any consequence of the reader acting on the information in this book. If in doubt, we recommend that you speak to a qualified professional. To the best of our knowledge all information is correct at the time of print (June 2013).

Contents

Dionne

'I don't want my mum to know'

Age: 17

Dionne lives with her mum and has just started studying for her 'A' levels at a local college. She has been seeing a lad called Lee, who is 22, for a few months – but she sees this as a casual thing at the moment.

Dionne's best mate is her friend from school, Jane. Jane went with Dionne to her local clinic where the pregnancy test was carried out.

Dionne's thoughts

- What's Mum going to say?
- Will I have to give up college?
- Where will I live?
- Is Lee going to stick around?
- Where am I going to get money from?
- Shall I keep it?
- Where can I get advice from?
- How will it affect Mum and Dad?
- If I decide to keep it, what or how should I tell my mum?
- I'm scared of going to the clinic – what will they ask me?
- How far gone am I?
- Am I going to get fat?

Sarah

'How will I cope?'

Age: 15

Sarah lives with her mum but stays at her boyfriend's house a lot. Her mum isn't home much and they don't have a great relationship. She's been with her boyfriend, Jamie, for 9 months.

Sarah had a one night stand with a lad called Frank, but she is not sure if Frank or Jamie is the father of the baby. Her best friend is Jess. Sarah bought a pregnancy test kit from the pound shop when she thought she might be pregnant.

Sarah's thoughts

- What will my friends say?
- Will I finish my exams?
- What will people think of our family?
- Should I tell Jamie about my one night stand?
- How will I find out who the father is?
- Shall I keep it?
- What about school?
- Where will I get support?
- What support (if any) will I get from my mum?
- What will people think of me?
- Will my friends want to know me?
- What's going to happen to me?
- When will people notice?
- What about my figure?
- Where will I live?

9

Louise

'Am I ready for this?'

Age: 20

Louise lives in her own flat by herself and has a long-term relationship with her boyfriend John, who is 26 and is quite supportive.

She works full time and was thinking about some training that her workplace had offered her. However, Louise found out she was pregnant.

Louise lives a long way from her friends and family and isn't in regular contact with them. Her friends are either from Uni or live at home, back in Wolverhampton. She gets on well with her mum but she's not that friendly with her step dad. Louise confirmed she was pregnant with a pregnancy test kit from the chemist.

Louise's thoughts

- What is John going to say?
- Shall we keep it?
- Will this change everything I had planned in life?
- Will I be able to adapt and change?
- Should I go back to work when the baby's old enough?
- How much will work pay me if I am on maternity leave – and for how long?
- Can John support all three of us?
- Will I find it hard to lose weight after the pregnancy?

You

'What's your story?'

We're sure the stories on the three previous pages have one or two things in common with yours. We're also sure that in some ways you feel a bit differently to them. So what is your story? Jot down a few notes below to compare, it may help you think a little more clearly...

Name .... Age...

Due date ....

Hospital/birthplace ....

Midwife name and no. ....

Top name choice (Boy) ....(Girl).......................................

Where will you live? ....

What plans do you have after you've had your baby?

....

....

....

....

....

....

....

....

....

What future hopes do you have for your child?

....

....

....

....

....

....

....

....

....

What other thoughts and questions do you have? It may be helpful to jot them down here, ready to ask your midwife or doctor.

....

....

....

....

....

....

....

....

....

Trimesters

Pregnancy is usually grouped into three-month periods called trimesters. During each trimester your baby is developing significantly and each trimester represents a certain milestone in your pregnancy. A full-term pregnancy lasts between 37 and 41 weeks.

dr. roberts

Weeks 1–5

The early weeks of a baby's development are really important. Many women are unaware that they are pregnant. You may experience a lot of tiredness.

Weeks 6–12

WEEKS	BABY	YOU	SELF-HELP IDEAS
6	Baby's heart is the size of a small seed. Brain and spine are starting to develop.	You may have noticed your breasts are more sensitive or are bigger.	Confirm your pregnancy with a pregnancy test. A first morning urine test may be more accurate. Make an appointment with a midwife or GP. Start taking folic acid 400mcg daily until the 12th week of your pregnancy, if you're not already doing so.
7-10	Baby's face is forming. Baby's heart is beating. At 9 weeks the baby is 2cm in length.	You may feel tired or sick. You may need to wee more often.	Rest. Drink plenty of fluids. Eat little and often, try ginger biscuits to help you stop feeling sick, or dry toast. Meet your midwife.
11-12	Baby is fully formed, 8cm. Baby is sucking and swallowing.	Waist getting bigger, a line may form from your belly button to your pubic bone = linea nigra. May make more vaginal discharge.	Wear more comfortable clothing. Buy bigger sizes instead of maternity wear. Check that you have a scan appointment.

Centimetres

0 1 2 3 4 5 6 7 8 9 10 11 12 13 14 15

Trimesters

WEEKS	BABY	YOU	SELF-HELP IDEAS
13	Your placenta has grown enough to continue your pregnancy. Your baby's systems are starting to function, but you will still supply important nutrients and oxygen. They move from your bloodstream, through the placenta, to your baby.	Your tiredness and sickness should get better. You may feel relieved that the first 12 weeks have passed. Your midwife should just be able to feel your baby through your stomach. You could need the toilet more as your growing baby may press on your bladder.	Rest when you can. Eat a balanced diet. You may be able to apply for **Healthy Start,** which allows you to exchange vouchers for milk or fruit and veg. See page 71. Make decisions regarding your screening blood tests, which should have been explained by your midwife.
14-17	The baby has its own set of fingerprints. Fingernails and toenails are growing and it has a firm hand grip.	You may start to feel sensations of flutters, bubbles popping or tapping as you begin to identify the baby's movements.	Visit your dentist for a free check-up.
18-20	The baby begins to lay down fat deposits under the skin.	Almost halfway there. You may develop dark patches called **CHLOASMA** and stretch marks may start to appear.	Get fitted for a support bra. You should be getting ready for your second detailed scan, which checks your baby's body is developing properly.
21-24	Baby's ears begin to develop and your baby is covered in fine hair called **LANUGO.** The baby has teeth and hair. It can suck its thumb and can now hiccup. The baby is approx. 27cm long.	Your baby is moving more and more strongly.	Let your employer know when you plan to leave work.
25-28	The baby can hear and respond to your voice. The baby's muscles and organs grow rapidly. The brain carries on maturing. Opens its eyelids for the first time.	Talk to your baby and play it your favourite song. Monitor the baby's movements.	You will be checked for anaemia. See your midwife for a **MATB1** certificate to give to your employer.

16 17 18 19 20 21 22 23 24 25 26 27 28 29 30 3

Weeks 29–41

You may be able to apply for a Sure Start grant now. See page 73.

Trimesters

WEEKS	BABY	YOU	SELF-HELP IDEAS
29	When stretched out the baby could measure 42cm from top to toe.	You may experience backache. You may notice mini contractions, which are normal – they are called Braxton Hicks. Keep talking to your baby.	Get someone to massage your back. Check your posture. Aquanatal classes are wonderful to ease backache. Start packing your bag for hospital. Attend antenatal classes.
31-33	Even if your baby is born prematurely now, they have a much better chance of survival at this stage. The baby's head size is in proportion to the rest of its body.	You may notice increased vaginal discharge, so wear a pad.	Pack your bag ready to take to the hospital, as the baby could come any time from now. Keep a taxi number and some spare cash to hand.
34-36	The baby may begin the journey of moving down into your pelvis, if it is your first baby = engagement.	Hormones relax your pelvic ligaments so you may feel some discomfort. You may feel as if the pregnancy has dropped = lightening. This gives you more room and so you may feel less breathless.	Try gentle rocking movements of your pelvis. Lie on your left-hand side whenever possible to enable the baby to get into the right position for labour. Complete the birth plan.
37-41	The baby is putting on one ounce per day. The baby is forming a black green mucous plug called meconium, which will be their first nappy poo.	You may be seen more frequently by your midwife, especially if this is you first baby. Your cervix is slowly changing, ready for labour. You may have a few false alarms.	Only a few babies arrive on their due date, it's normal for them to be up to 2 weeks (or even longer!) overdue. Rest where possible. Try not to be too impatient, **you're almost there!**

2 33 34 35 36 37 38 39 40 41 42 43 44 45 46 47

Health

Diet

During pregnancy it is important that you eat a **balanced diet.** A mother's diet is the foundation to her baby's development. Each nutrient you eat is vital in the baby's growth. These nutrients are:

dionne

PROTEIN
Eat 2–3 portions daily

CALCIUM
Eat 3 portions a day

CARBOHYDRATES
Eat 1 portion at each meal

VITAMINS
Eat 5 portions of fruit and veg per day

FAT
(and sugar)
Keep to a minimum

You should include each of these in **EVERY** meal.

Proteins consist of:

- Red meat
- Eggs
- Green leafy vegetables (e.g. spinach)
- Pulses and beans (e.g. kidney beans)
- Oily fish (e.g. sardines – limit to 2 portions per week, they can contain too much mercury which can be harmful to your baby)

You are encouraged to eat **5 portions of fruit and vegetables in one day.** A glass of orange juice is classed as 1 portion. A portion is roughly what would fit into the palm of your hand.

Carbohydrates consist of:

- Rice
- Potato
- Pasta
- Bread

Try wholemeal varieties which are healthier and help with constipation.

Fats

Healthy fats are found in olive oil and vegetable oils.

16

Calcium **If possible drink 6–8 glasses of water a day.**

During pregnancy it is important to have a healthy balanced diet. Calcium in particular is important to produce strong bones and healthy teeth. This can be found in milk, cheese and other dairy products.

If you don't like milk-based products, substitute with broccoli, raisins, dried apricots or spinach.

Vitamins

If you need **supplements** take **pregnancy preparations** as these have the correct dose of vitamins and minerals. **Speak to your midwife, GP or pharmacist.**

Folic acid is essential for development of the spine and nervous system, and should be taken especially in the first 12 weeks when the baby is developing.

Just remember you may be able to claim Healthy Start. See page 71.

Iron-rich foods are vital to carry extra oxygen to the baby. These include:

- Dark green vegetables (e.g. cabbage, peas)
- Fortified breakfast cereals (e.g. Weetabix)
- Eggs (well-cooked)
- Dried fruit (e.g. apricots)

MELON is rich in vitamins A and C, which are good for you.

WEIGHT GAIN IN PREGNANCY IS ON AVERAGE **10–12.5 kg** (22–28 lbs)

Louise

Avoid foods such as pate and blue vein cheeses or mould ripened crusted cheeses such as brie and stilton.

There is a risk of getting an infection called listeria, which is linked to stillbirth, miscarriage and abnormalities.

Also avoid

- **Homemade mayonnaise**
- **Soft eggs** (risk of salmonella)
- **Liver** (contains too much vitamin A, which can be toxic)
- **Shellfish** (can be contaminated with bacteria)
- **Limit tuna** (2 portions per week)

STOP

Crave toothpaste!?

Some people crave things like fried chicken, cheesy crisps and SOIL!

Cravings are said to occur due to hormonal influences that affect your tastes and smell (however, some people say that cravings reflect a dietary imbalance and it is a message from your body telling you what you may be lacking).

If you crave cheese this may indicate a calcium deficiency. Try broccoli or green veg as a low-fat alternative.

TRUE or FALSE?

We've all heard the different stories and myths surrounding pregnancy.

But which are true and false?

TRUE: If you have a known nut allergy in your family we recommend that you avoid any nuts. Peanuts should generally be avoided as anything you eat can cross over in the placenta and we do not want the baby to become too sensitised to nuts when they are in the womb.

I was told to avoid peanuts in my diet.

FALSE: Coffee, tea and chocolate contain a chemical called caffeine, which is a stimulant. Excessive amounts can lead to miscarriage or low birth weight babies. Cola also contains caffeine. Allow up to 200mg per day, e.g. 2 **mugs of instant coffee** (100mg each). Or 2 **mugs of tea** (75mg each). N.B. One can of cola is 40mg. Did you know that tea and coffee contain a chemical called **tanin** which stops you from getting enough **iron**. Drink a glass of orange juice instead.

Am I allowed as much coffee as I like?

Am I eating for two?

FALSE: Think of the pounds you need to shed after the baby! Avoid too much fatty, sugary food, e.g. crisps, chips and pastries. The idea is to have quality foods instead of quantity – everything in moderation.

For more information and advice about food visit **eatwell.gov.uk** and **food.gov.uk**

LIGHT MEALS and SNACK SUGGESTIONS

Soup and a bread roll

Dried fruit raisins, apricots, pumpkin seeds

Smoothie/ milkshake: Disguise fruit in milk or natural yoghurt, e.g. bananas, strawberries and mangoes. Spoil yourself and add a scoop of ice-cream.

dionne

Potato Baked with a variety of fillings such as tuna, sweetcorn, cheese or beans

Pitta bread pockets with ham and salad

Fruit salad bananas in particular are high-energy foods full of potassium and B vitamins

Vegetable sticks and dips carrot, celery, sweet pepper, cucumber or courgette with humous

Salad and an omelette watercress is especially high in iron, garnish with spinach leaves

Baked beans on toast or **cheese on toast**

Did you know that when preparing food you need to be aware of the following?

HANDWASHING and HYGIENE

- Wash hands before handling food.
- Cook raw meat and poultry thoroughly.
- Bacteria multiplies rapidly in the right conditions.
- Always store food at the appropriate temperature.
- Wear gloves for gardening and handling cat litter. This avoids the transmission of a parasite called toxoplasmosis, found in soil and cat faeces.
- Salmonella can be transmitted if you do not wash your fruit and vegetables.
- Reheat any food thoroughly until piping hot throughout.
- Check sell by dates on cook chill foods.
- Check manufacturer's instructions on cooking ready meals.

For more information visit **eatwell.gov.uk**

> I was really shocked to find out that drinking alcohol could affect the development of my unborn baby. I saw this on a poster at the hospital.

dionne

> What's really scary is nobody really knows how much alcohol you would have to drink to cause Foetal Alcohol Syndrome, which can cause abnormalities like small head, cleft lip and palate, short slit eyes, stunted growth, learning disabilities.

You are strongly advised to avoid alcohol completely whilst pregnant to cut down the risks to your baby.

Some alternative recipes

Apple Zing – Serves 2
2 apples, 1 medium can of pineapple juice, 12 ice cubes, 2 tbsp of fresh orange juice

Pina Colada – Serves 3
Pineapple and coconut juice, 12 ice cubes, 1 scoop of ice cream, half cup of whole milk

Strawberry De-lish – Serves 1
1 large ripe mango, half punnet of strawberries, 1 banana, ice

Oranberry Mix – Serves 1
Simply half orange juice and half cranberry juice!

Method for all
Add all ingredients and blend until smooth. Serve and enjoy!

Try to avoid too many sweets and fizzy drinks as they are not good for your teeth.

Did you know it's really important to look after your teeth and gums while you're pregnant? **See below for WHY.**

Eating foods that are full of calcium, like milk and yoghurt, will really help as the growing baby zaps your calcium reserves from your teeth and bones!

MILK

Bleeding and swollen gums are often common complaints. Hormones are responsible for some of the symptoms you may experience. For example, hormones cause gums to become soft and spongy, so bacteria and plaque deposits can build up.

Most dental treatment is safe while you are pregnant. It is recommend that any **amalgam fillings** are done after the baby is born. If emergency treatment is needed then your dentist may be able to offer a safer alternative.

midwife

You should visit your dentist and get a check-up.

Not everybody likes the dentist but if you leave things they'll just get worse. **It's free if you are an NHS patient,** hold an exemption certificate and continue to do so, up until your child is a year old.

Fact

Did you know there is almost as much sugar in a bag of fruit gum type sweets as there is **IN A BAG OF SUGAR?!**

SUGAR

Paracetamol

Always check with the pharmacist before you buy any over the counter medicines or painkillers.

Natural products

- Even herbal/natural tablets can be harmful. You should always ask a pharmacist, doctor or midwife before taking anything.
- Be careful when using aromatherapy products or oils when pregnant – check with a qualified herbalist or aromatherapist first.

The normal dose is 2 tablets every 4–6 hours.

Painkillers are not recommended during pregnancy; however, paracetamol is OK very occasionally. If you find yourself needing painkillers regularly speak to your midwife or GP.

Remember your body's own natural painkillers – 'endorphins'.

Try using a hot water bottle, massage or a warm bath to ease any pain.

Recreational drugs

Cocaine/crack

Both of these are illegal Class A drugs. They can cause liver damage, miscarriage, stillbirth, premature baby, lower appetite, reduced sleep and there is always a risk of overdose.

For more information contact FRANK at www.talktofrank.com or call free on 0800 77 6600.

If you feel that you have a problem with drugs it may be possible to quit with specialised support. **Speak to your midwife.**

Cannabis

- Cannabis is still an illegal drug. If mixed with tobacco it has the same damaging affect as smoking.
- Even if not mixed with tobacco, cannabis has more tar and carcinogens than tobacco.
- Research is yet to be done on its effects as a drug.
- It is a depressant and can cause memory loss, anxiety, depression and paranoia.
- For more information visit **www.knowcannabis.org.uk** or phone FRANK free on 0800 77 6600.

What's in a cigarette?

A 20 a day smoker can spend up to £210 a month on cigarettes.

All gone up in smoke!

Think of how much money you could save!

Think of what you could spend the money on!

ACETONE
nail varnish remover

BENZENE
petrol fumes

HYDROGEN SULPHIDE
stink bomb gas

TOLUENE
industrial solvent

RADON
radioactive gas

POLONIUM 210
radioactive fallout

LEAD
batteries

DDT
insecticide

sarah

45080 0960

If you feel you need some support to give up smoking **speak to your midwife** or contact **the NHS Stop Smoking Service at www.smokefree.nhs.uk or call 0800 022 4 332.**

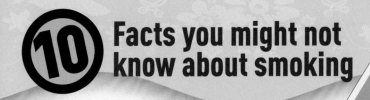

⑩ Facts you might not know about smoking

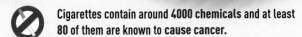 Cigarettes contain around **4000 chemicals** and at least 80 of them are known to **cause cancer.**

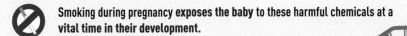 Smoking during pregnancy **exposes the baby to these harmful chemicals** at a vital time in their development.

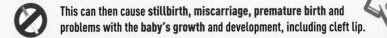 This can then cause **stillbirth, miscarriage, premature birth** and problems with the **baby's growth** and development, including cleft lip.

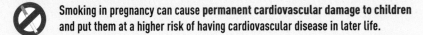 Smoking in pregnancy can cause **permanent cardiovascular damage to children** and put them at a higher risk of having cardiovascular disease in later life.

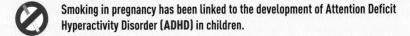 Smoking in pregnancy has been linked to the development of Attention Deficit Hyperactivity Disorder (**ADHD**) in children.

⊘ Smoking causes **premature ageing, i.e. wrinkles and dry coarse hair,** as well as **bad breath,** yellow teeth and unhealthy gums.

⊘ **Secondhand smoke** is also very harmful, up to 75% of this smoke is spread into the air and **can cause cot death,** respiratory infections and ear infections in babies.

⊘ **Stopping smoking at any time** during your pregnancy will increase your chances of having a **healthier baby.**

⊘ The NHS **Stop Smoking Service, Smokefree,** offers support for pregnant women and their partners, family and friends in a variety of venues including your own home, GP surgery, pharmacy or community venue.

⊘ **Smokefree** can advise on behaviour change and **offer treatments** such as patches, gum and inhalators.

 **SMOKE FREE**

Are non-judgemental
Don't tell you what to do
Listen to what you say

Feelings

During your pregnancy you may experience a rollercoaster of emotions.

Early pregnancy

To start with I didn't want to believe I was pregnant, as I hadn't planned it this way. I began to get used to the idea once I was over the initial shock, and then I felt excited.

dionne

I felt really happy to begin with but then started to worry about having a miscarriage. I felt better once I got past 12 weeks as my midwife said after 12 weeks miscarriage is less likely to happen.

sarah

Being pregnant and the way this makes you and your partner feel can affect your relationship. My partner John is supportive but sometimes partners can become aggressive or violent and may threaten to harm you or the baby. If you think this may be happening to you there is something you can do about it:

louise

I was all over the place – my moods changed from day to day – but Mum told me this was normal. Apparently it's caused by your hormones during pregnancy.

- Tell your midwife or health visitor (ask to see them on their own) if your partner threatens you, hits you, damages property, locks you up or keeps money from you.

- In an emergency you should ring the police (999).

- Call the National Domestic Violence helpline on 0808 2000 247 for advice and support.

During/mid pregnancy

I started to worry that something might be wrong with the baby, like an abnormality. I was having really vivid dreams and I would wake up feeling certain something was wrong. I felt silly telling anyone but once I told my midwife she reassured me that lots of other women felt like this too.

louise

I felt really down at 4 months and just didn't know why – I soon realised I was not alone. When I told my midwife she was really supportive and suggested some things I could try when I felt low, such as 'me' time, relaxing and pampering myself.

dionne

sarah

I started attending antenatal classes. This really helped me as I met other mums to be and shared stories with them – it was good as we helped support each other.

Late pregnancy

Towards the end of my pregnancy I started to get really scared about actually giving birth to my baby – it is natural to feel like this. I got a lot of help from the group and my midwife, who told me the more you can prepare yourself the easier it will be. You will also feel more in control, which is really important when you are younger than other mums.

dionne's friend Jane

I remember in the last few weeks of my pregnancy I was really fed up and just felt huge and really uncomfortable. Everybody kept telling me to rest – I wish I had, because once the baby arrived there wasn't much chance to rest at all!

dionne's mum

Antenatal Care

The hand-held maternity notes that you will put together with your midwife will hold essential information about you and your pregnancy. It is important that you carry these notes around with you all the time, e.g. if you go on holiday or if you go out. Remember that your notes will be understood by any maternity team.

sarah's friend jess

Your midwife will take a booking history which usually contains information about:

- Personal information, e.g. DOB, contact details
- Your past/current medical history
- Your past pregnancies

She will also discuss your birthing options, i.e. where you would like to deliver such as at the hospital, at home or in a birthing unit.

Screening tests during pregnancy consist of:

- A/N blood tests, e.g. HIV or sickle cell
- Urine (wee) tests
- Blood pressure readings
- Checking the stomach

Don't forget... write down any worries or concerns and ask your midwife when you see her.

You should also receive advice and information about your pregnancy.

ABBREVIATIONS

Sometimes you may not understand the medical jargon that is written in your notes. Here are some common examples and what they stand for. Ask your midwife to explain any you don't understand.

AFP	The AFP test detects the level of alpha-fetoprotein (a protein made by the baby) in your blood
AN	Antenatal
ANC	Antenatal Clinic
ARM	Artificial Rupture of Membranes – when the midwife breaks your waters for you
BP	Blood Pressure
Br	Breech – baby is lying bottom down
Cx	Cervix
CTG	Cardiotocograph – tracing of the baby's heart-beat on a monitor
Ceph	Baby is head down
DFM	Diminished Foetal Movements – your baby's movements are less frequent
EDD	Estimated Due Date of delivery – calculated by adding 9 months and 7 days to the date of conception
FHHR	Foetal Heart Heard Regular – measured on a hand-held monitor or with a Pinard's Trumpet (right)
FMF	Foetal Movement Felt – baby's movement may have been felt
Hb	Haemoglobin – the red blood cells that carry oxygen around the body and bind to iron
Height of the fundus	The fundus is the top of the womb – the midwife monitors the growth of your baby by measuring from the top of the fundus to the top of the pubic bone, which should match the stage of the pregnancy you are meant to be at
IOL	Induction of Labour – artificially starting labour
LMP	Last Menstrual Period

LSCS	Lower Segment Caesarean Section – an operation that uses surgery to remove the baby from the womb
MSU	Mid-Stream Urine specimen – this is sent to the lab for testing
Multigravida	A woman who has been pregnant before
NAD	No Abnormalities Detected – all is normal and well
Oedema	Swelling of hands or feet
PET	Pre-Eclampsia Toxaemia – a potentially serious condition in pregnancy affecting your blood pressure, which needs to be closely monitored
pp to the brim	How much of the baby's head is present in relation to the brim of the pelvis. The baby's head is divided into fifths, e.g. 3/5 palpable means 3 parts of the head can be felt and the remaining 2/5 are still in the pelvis
Primigravida	A woman who is pregnant for the first time
SROM	Spontaneous Rupture of Membranes – your waters break naturally
Trace	A small amount
USS	Ultrasound Scan
UTI	Urinary Tract Infection – water infection
VE	Vaginal Examination
30 + 4	30 weeks and 4 days gestation

midwife

If it is your first pregnancy your midwife may see you more often when you get to about 36 weeks.

If your pregnancy is straightforward with no complications, your midwife will provide most of your care. Make sure you have all the necessary contact numbers if you need to get in touch with a health professional or the hospital.

Birth Plan

This is... ...where you consider your options for your delivery. The midwife looking after you will always hope to respect your wishes as best she can, but no one knows how your labour will go. Try to keep it brief and realistic.

It is not fixed and can be changed.

It's about a two-way communication between yourself and the midwife looking after you.

midwife

When Filled in during the antenatal period with your birth partner.

It is then worth discussing it with your community midwife.

Where Usually written in your hand-held maternity notes or you may prefer to write it separately.

What... ...does it contain? Here are some examples:

- Choice of birth partner
- Can other people be present – e.g. students
- Choice of pain relief
- Birth position
- Environment – music, dim lights, etc.
- When the baby is born – cutting the cord
- Baby placed on to your tummy straight after delivery for skin-to-skin contact

louise's boyfriend john

See what you need to pack on page 52.

Scans and Tests

ULTRASOUND SCAN

Dating scan 10–14 weeks

At this stage the sonographer is scanning to:

- Estimate your due date
- See if there is more than one baby present!

Detailed scan 18–23 weeks

At this stage the sonographer is scanning to:

- Detect any physical problems
- Check the baby's growth and position
- Check the position of the placenta

Involves a **sonographer** (person trained to scan you and explain what the scan shows) applying gel and rolling a probe over your tummy, which provides a picture of your baby.

You may have to have some extra scans if the midwife or consultant is concerned about the size or position of your baby, or if you are having twins.

dr. roberts (trained sonographer)

BLOOD TESTS

There are a variety of blood tests performed at different stages of your pregnancy. Here are some examples of those tests:

Checks for blood group
Can be rhesus negative or positive

Checks for hepatitis B
Your baby will need to be vaccinated at birth if test is positive

Checks for syphilis
Can cause damage to your baby but treated with antibiotics if detected

Checks for full blood count
Checks to see if you have a lack of iron

Checks for German measles
Checks for immunity

Checks for HIV
Active care in pregnancy can reduce the chances of it passing to the baby

dionne's friend Jane

Every pregnant mother worries about the health of her unborn baby. As part of your antenatal care you will be offered different tests, which are done for different reasons.

It is important that you know which tests are being offered, and you may need to talk to your partner or family. Remember to ask your midwife for further explanation if there is anything you do not understand.

midwife

Screening test
(routine)

Non-invasive
What does this mean?

Can be a scan or a blood test and is called an AFP test (see page 29).

Done between 16 and 20 weeks to detect Down's Syndrome.

Only gives an indication.
This test will give a 'risk' result.

If high risk, a diagnostic test is offered.

Diagnostic test

Invasive
What does this mean?

Only offered if the screening test gives a 'high risk' result.

Fluid samples (amniocentesis) or tissue is taken from around the baby (chorionic villi).

The tests increase the risk of miscarriage and the sample results can take a couple of weeks.

You may also be offered a detailed anatomy scan.

Points to consider Do you know...?

- ✒ What the test involves – is it a screening or diagnostic test?
- ✒ The length of time to get the results?
- ✒ How will you receive the results?
- ✒ What will be your options if you get a 'high risk' result?
- ✒ Who will be able to support you if this is the situation – where to go to next?
- ✒ You have a choice as to whether you take any test offered.

Tests
Chorionic villi
Sampling is done at 10–13 weeks
Amniocentesis
Sampling is done at around 16 weeks

Minor Symptoms
of Pregnancy

Headaches
- Drink plenty of fluids and get fresh air
- Paracetamol if needed, cool compress pads, rest
- If symptoms persist see your midwife

Mood swings

Bleeding gums
- See a dentist – it's FREE
- Brush teeth with a soft brush

Heartburn
- Eat little and often
- Avoid spicy foods
- Drink milk and try indigestion remedies

Tiredness
- Check that you're not anaemic
- Have regular rest periods

Backache
- Use a hot water bottle and massage
- Watch posture and sit with a cushion
- Warm bath

Tender breasts
- Wear a supportive bra

Nausea/vomiting
- Avoid fatty foods
- Try ginger tea or biscuits
- Try fruit or herbal teas
- Eat slowly
- Try acupressure wristbands used for travelling

Constipation and piles
- Eat plenty of fruit and veg
- Drink plenty of fluids
- Review if taking iron supplements
- Use creams and gels

Stretch marks
- Moisturise skin

Thrush
- Wear cotton knickers and see your GP for treatment

Varicose veins
- Wear support tights and take regular rest periods

Swollen ankles
- Put your feet up
- Wear sensible shoes

The hormones oestrogen, progesterone and relaxin cause the womb to grow. They have a relaxing and softening effect on all parts of the body, which slows all body systems down and can cause the above symptoms.

What to Look Out For

The Traffic Light System

Most of the following symptoms are common in pregnancy and are usually nothing to worry about, **but if you have them for a long time or they are very troublesome, talk to your midwife about them.**

RED	AMBER	GREEN
Warning, danger, contact doctor or hospital straight away	Be careful, get a check-up as soon as possible	Common – relax but be aware

Nausea and vomiting

During the first 12 weeks of pregnancy some women experience nausea due to the high levels of hormones supporting the pregnancy.

However, persistent vomiting (being sick again and again) could be a sign of **hyperemesis gravidarum**. This can affect how you feel on a daily basis. If left this could potentially lead to dehydration (which means you are very low on fluids). Some symptoms you would see or experience are:

- Urine is dark and small amounts, may smell strong
- Not keeping down any liquids or foods
- Weight loss
- Dizziness

If you have these symptoms, you may need to be assessed in hospital by a doctor.

Arm/finger pains

You may experience tight puffy tingling feelings in your hands. This may indicate **carpal tunnel syndrome.** Lift your arms above your head to help drain the fluid, especially first thing in the morning and last thing at night. Also try shaking your hands.

If this persists you should see the physiotherapist, who may advise you to **wear hand braces.** All these symptoms will only be temporary throughout your pregnancy.

Breathlessness

Can be caused by anaemia (not having enough iron) or your growing bump pushing up on your diaphragm (lower part of your lungs).

Be aware of sudden chest pain that may be accompanied by calf pain. This could indicate a condition called **pulmonary embolism**, i.e. blood clots on the lungs. You need to seek urgent medical advice.

Bleeding

Any bleeding during pregnancy should be checked by your doctor.

Leg pain

If you have a hot, tender, red calf, which causes difficulty in standing or walking on that leg, you need to seek urgent medical attention.

health visitor

Itching

Can occur especially when your skin gets dry and stretches during your pregnancy. This can get worse in the hot weather.

If you have very itchy hands and feet, particularly at night, you should tell your doctor or midwife as it could be a sign of illness (obstetric cholestasis).

Headaches

If you have very painful headaches, especially in the front of your head, flashing lights or spots before your eyes you should contact your doctor straight away. You may also have swelling of your hands, feet and face. This could be a sign that your blood pressure is getting too high (pre-eclampsia).

louise

Abdominal pain

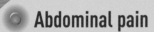

This may be important, especially if it is very painful and/or accompanied by bleeding. Contact your doctor or hospital.

Diminished Foetal Movements
DFM

You will become familiar with your baby's pattern of moving or kicking, especially after the 28th week of pregnancy. You should feel at least 10 kicks or movements in any 12-hour period (when you are awake). If you notice fewer movements or changes, you should let your hospital know as they may need to monitor the baby.

Breast-feeding

What are breasts for?

Breasts are for breastfeeding but they are also an important part of your relationship with your partner.

I was really unsure about breast feeding, **I was actually really embarrassed** by the whole idea of **getting my boobs out in public.**

More celebrities do it now, like Angelina Jolie, Victoria Beckham and Beyoncé.

But it doesn't have to be like that, you can be **discrete** and use a **blanket, scarf or muslin square** to cover yourself. There are also lots of places that support breastfeeding mums.

If you want to breastfeed it is important that you get as much support as possible. Learn as much as you can about how breastfeeding works during your pregnancy. If you go to a group you'll get support from other young mums, or you can ask your midwife for more information.

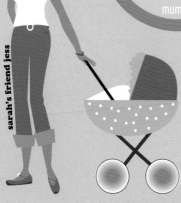

sarah's friend jess

So how does it all work?

- The breast works on a supply and demand basis – the more you feed the more your breast makes milk.
- Babies take as much milk as they need at each feed.
- Breast milk changes to meet the demands of your baby.
- If you are relaxed and happy, your milk will flow more.
- Night feeding is important, especially in the early weeks, to help with your milk supply.

The benefits of breastfeeding

For your baby...

The old saying 'breast is best' is very true as breast milk contains everything a growing baby needs. It's full of nutrients and antibodies which will help your baby fight off infection.

Breastfed babies are less likely to develop certain conditions as they get older, such as: asthma, eczema, diabetes and obesity

For mum...

It can help to protect you from developing breast and ovarian cancer and the bone disease osteoporosis.

Breastfeeding helps you to lose weight and get your shape back as you'll burn more calories whilst breastfeeding (up to 500 calories a day). Sounds better than jogging in the park!

Breastfeeding is FREE, saving you hundreds of pounds a year. It is also convenient and exactly the right temperature!

41

The beginning

As soon as your baby is born you should hold them next to your breasts. Your baby's instincts will help it to nuzzle and latch on to the breast. Feeding your baby within the first hour gets breast-feeding off to a good start.

Ask your midwife to help you with latching your baby on to the breast. You can either feed your baby sitting them up or lying them down. Remember that breast-feeding should not hurt!

Colostrum

This is the milk produced in the first few days – it is very important, like 'liquid gold'. It has important antibodies to protect your baby from infection and disease. It contains all the nutrients your baby needs and a small amount is enough for the first few weeks.

Remember your baby's stomach is the size of a small cherry tomato at this stage!

Colostrum helps to get rid of the first poo, which is called meconium.

The early days

Breastfeeding should be baby led, i.e. babies feed when they want to.

Another name for this is demand feeding.

Make sure you get plenty of rest and support from your partner/family as you will need to concentrate on the feeding.

Eat little and often. You may also feel that you are more thirsty.

'When your milk comes in'
This usually occurs between days 4 and 7 and is hormonally related. Your baby may feed for longer periods but less often. Your baby should produce 6–8 wet nappies in 24 hours.

dionne's friend Jane

health visitor

Remember, your milk changes to meet the demands of your growing baby!

SUPPORT Get support from your health visitor and local breastfeeding support groups in your area.

Try finding a local breastfeeding support group at www.netmums.com

Sterilisation

Up until a baby's first year of life it is important that you sterilise their feeding equipment. This is because they are very sensitive to germs and infections.

health visitor

Wash the bottles in hot soapy water using a bottle brush. You should remove every particle of milk. Constantly check that the teats are not cracked or split. If they are throw them away immediately.

You can't stop your baby coming in to contact with germs, especially when they start moving around and putting everything in their mouths, but one way that you can reduce the risk is by sterilising.

There are different methods of sterilisation

✤ Cold water   ✤ Microwave   ✤ Boiling   ✤ Steam

DO

- Try to keep a clean area in your kitchen for sterilising.
- Wash the bottles in hot soapy water using a bottle brush. You should remove every particle of milk. Remember to rinse the items well.
- Follow the manufacturer's instructions regarding the sterilisation process.
- Wash your hands very well before you begin to touch any sterilised items.
- Keep sterilising solutions out of the reach of children.

DON'T

- Don't use any split or damaged teats. Throw them away.
- Don't pick up sterilised teats with your fingers. Use tongs if you have them.
- Do not re-use any leftover milk. If it hasn't been used within an hour of a feed throw it away.
- Don't put metal items in microwaves or microwave sterilisers.
- Don't make up feeds in batches and store in your fridge. Make each feed as you need it.
- Don't warm any feeds in the microwave.

Questions and Answers

Some suggestions

Aquanatal classes

Classes may run at your local swimming baths. They are relaxing and brilliant for relieving backache and stretching your body ready for labour.

Yoga and Pilates

Exercise like yoga and Pilates helps to keep your joints and muscles more flexible. They also...

- Strengthen your pelvic floor (the muscles which are stretched when you're in labour)
- Increase your understanding of how your body works
- Help you to relax

dr. roberts

Walking

It's free, and is an easy form of exercise which is good for your circulation.

Avoid contact sports
such as martial arts or football.
Also avoid fairground rides.

Do not lie flat on your back from 28 weeks onwards.

Remember to warm up first, cool down after, and stretch.

dionne

How much exercise am I allowed to do now that I am pregnant?

If you didn't run marathons before, don't start now! Do what you would normally do but don't start any hard exercises.

Listen to your body as it's a good indicator as to how you feel. If you do too much your stomach may react by tightening, leading to Braxton Hicks contractions. If you carry on doing the activity these could become stronger or you may become dizzy.

If you have had a miscarriage before you may want to avoid any exercise, especially during the early stages of your pregnancy.

If you have an exercise instructor it's important to tell them that you are pregnant so allowances can be made. Also take regular rest periods and stop if you feel unwell.

Can I dye my hair while I am pregnant?

louise

midwife

YOU CAN.
Tell your hairdresser you're pregnant, but be mindful that your hair colour may not come out as you expected due to your pregnancy hormones, which can cause a different reaction. Try a patch test first in an area that you can't see. Some hairdressers may not accept responsibility for the end result of your hair colour.

My friends say that there is no point in going to antenatal classes. Is this true?

Partners are welcome too.
Topics covered can include feelings, pregnancy health, pain relief, life with your baby, relaxation, tour of the labour ward and breastfeeding.

These classes may also be advertised as 'parentcraft'. They are just as important as your antenatal check-ups and cover all you need to know about your pregnancy. Classes are usually held in hospital or locally. Going to them gives you a chance for your questions to be answered, meaning you feel less worried. Make time for them – remember, your friends' or family's knowledge, no matter how useful, does not give the full picture. Books and DVDs are also useful but classes allow you to meet women who may be due around the same time as you, so you are likely to share common experiences. You may hear the answer to a question you wanted to ask.

midwife

dionne's friend Jane

I really enjoyed the classes and found out things I'd never have known – it was nice to meet other mums to be too.

What is the 'bleed' you get after the baby is born?

This is called **LOCHIA**. Once the afterbirth (placenta) has been delivered, the womb gradually shrinks back to its original size, and as this happens it sheds blood. The amount should lessen daily and can continue up to about 10–14 days. You will need to wear maternity towels. You should not use tampons – you will still feel uncomfortable and you may need to heal inside, so they could lead to an infection.

dr. roberts

sarah

My partner wants to have sex but I'm afraid that he will hurt the baby. What should I do?

It is important to realise that the baby is well-cushioned in your womb and that the neck of the womb is tightly closed. However, as you get bigger you may find lying on your back uncomfortable, so you may need to consider changing positions, e.g. being on top of your partner. Discuss your feelings with your partner and remember affection can be shown in other ways like kissing, cuddling and caressing. Although you can't get pregnant (as you already are), if you have a new sexual partner it's important to use a condom as you can still get a sexually transmitted infection (STI).

midwife

Can I wear my belly ring throughout my pregnancy?

YES YOU CAN.
If it becomes too tight as you grow bigger you may want to change it to a flexible plastic bar which moulds around your bump.

midwife

The show is a plug of mucus which sits at the neck of the womb. As you approach your due date, the neck of the womb is slowly getting ready for labour. As this occurs, some of the show may come away gradually. It is not a true sign of labour.

Do I have to get rid of my pet dog and cat while I am pregnant?

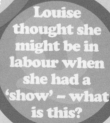

Louise thought she might be in labour when she had a 'show' – what is this?

NOT REALLY.
But avoid handling litter trays. If you have to, wear gloves. Cat faeces (poo) may contain a parasite which causes **TOXOPLASMOSIS.** This can be harmful to the baby. You should also be careful in the garden because the parasite can also be found in soil.

You should also wear gloves if 'poop scooping'. **Always** wash your hands afterwards. Do not leave your baby on its own in the room with a pet, as cats have been known to smother babies.

Avoid farms in the lambing season (higher risk of infections from sheep).

dr. roberts

louise's boyfriend john

48

Induction

dr. roberts

Some babies just don't want to come out, so you might need some **extra help** to get labour started. This is called **INDUCTION.** It usually happens when you've gone over your due date and the start of labour doesn't seem likely.

It can also be done if there is a problem with your pregnancy, e.g. the baby is not growing as well as it should be.

The doctor or midwife will check the cervix (neck of the womb) by doing a vaginal examination. Hopefully the cervix will be soft and beginning to open. If it isn't you may need some extra help.

Vaginal sweep

A VAGINAL SWEEP may be offered. This is where a midwife places a finger through the cervix and massages the area between the cervix and the membranes (sweeps). After, you may feel mild contractions as one of the labour hormones has been stimulated by the sweep. You may also have a slight spotting of blood.

Prostin method of induction

midwife

Prostin contains an artificial labour hormone called prostaglandin. In this method a vaginal tablet is inserted into the vagina to make it softer. You may need several doses, which are given 6 hours apart. The prostin may give you period-type pains. Both you and your baby will be checked regularly throughout this process. In between the doses you will be able to walk about and eat as normal.

49

When you need extra help

There are two ways of doing this:

1. You may need your waters broken. The ARM is the artificial rupture of membranes or 'breaking of waters'. This is where a crochet-type hook is passed through the neck of the womb opening to the membranes. Once there, the hook is used to break the membranes.

2. The drip method involves having an artificial hormone called syntocinon given slowly through a drip in your arm (after your waters have broken). This then causes contractions, so both you and your baby will need to be monitored.

dionne

Everyone is different and some inductions are lengthier than others. It's important that you and your partner get plenty of rest in case it takes a bit longer.

Reflexology

Reflexology is an alternative therapy where the sole of the foot is massaged. Some people believe it may help the cervix dilate, although this hasn't been proven.

You may need to attend a couple of sessions and it's usually offered from 38 weeks onwards. It may help you relax and feel good. You will need to check whether this service is offered at your unit.

Self-help techniques

It is said that some of the following may help kick-start your labour:

- 🔘 Have sex – sperm contains prostaglandin, which is one of the labour hormones.
- 🔘 Drink raspberry leaf tea after your 38th week of pregnancy.
- 🔘 Stimulate your nipples.
- 🔘 Eat a hot curry.

Having Your Baby

When to go into hospital

midwife

Your waters break

Sometimes it's difficult to tell if your waters have broken, as the waters are clear and do not smell. You may not even realise as it doesn't always gush out! For some people it just trickles.

Put a sanitary pad on and contact the hospital. The bag of water which surrounds your baby protects it against illness, so you will need to be monitored for signs of infection when you arrive at the hospital.

If the baby becomes distressed it may open its bowels (have a poo!). This would cause you to lose a black/green fluid, and needs immediate attention when you get to the hospital.

If your waters do go in a gush it may cause the baby's head to pass through the pelvis, causing it to turn or move, e.g. become breech (feet/bottom first). If this happens it could cause complications. For all of the reasons above it's important that you check in at the hospital now.

CONTRACTIONS

These are regular abdominal pains occurring at least twice every 10 minutes, for a good length of time. These are a good sign that you may be in labour. Each contraction should last for about 1 minute.

Louise and I made a list of all the things she might need before she went into hospital – hopefully this bag will be big enough to carry everything!

louise's boyfriend john

Also see the section on 'What to Look Out For' on page 37.

Hospital checklist

Tick the circles to check you have everything you need.

For Mum

Towels — Check

Baggy t-shirts (something used but comfortable) — Check

Your hospital notes — Check

Birth plan — Check

Hairbrush — Check

Toothbrush — Check

Lip balm — Check

Tissues — Check

Flannel — Check

Snack/food for partner — Check

Slippers — Check

Dressing gown — Check

Face spray (optional) — Check

Glucose or boiled sweets — Check

Magazine/book to read — Check

Clothes to go home in — Check

Camera/batteries — Check

Personal music player — Check

Drink/cordial — Check

Phone and charger — Check

Nightwear — Check

Disposable knickers — Check

Bras/breast pads — Check

Sanitary towels — Check

Pen and paper — Check

For Baby

Baby clothes including something warm for the baby to go home in — Check

Nappies and nappy sacks — Check

Small bottles cream/shampoo — Check

Mitts/shawl/hat/bibs — Check

Cotton wool and/or wipes — Check

Car seat to go home in — Check

Now, think about whether there is anything else that would be handy to include on YOUR checklist and add it below.

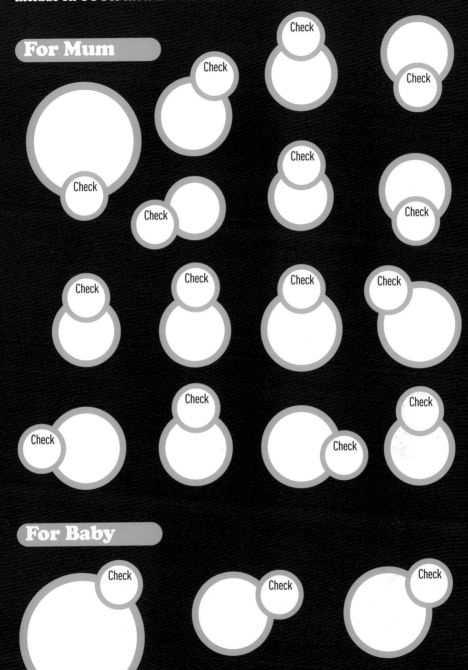

For Mum

Check

Check

Check

Check

Check

Check

Check

Check

Check

Check

Check

Check

Check

Check

Check

Check

For Baby

Check

Check

Check

Stages of labour

☆ Stage 1

Regular contractions allow the cervix to dilate to 10cm.

I'm getting bored in here, I'm ready to come out!

Contractions release hormones that help the labour to happen. Gravity helps speed things up, so staying upright and moving around is vital to shorten the labour. **For a first-time mother, this stage can last between 12 and 18 hours.**

At the transition stage the cervix is nearly open. Some mothers may become weepy, shaky, angry or sick. This marks the end of the first stage in preparation for the next stage.

Stage 2

This is when the baby **passes through the vagina, whilst you are pushing,** and makes an entry into the world. **Pushing can last between 1 and 2 hours.**

Stage 3

This involves the delivery of the afterbirth (placenta).

This process can take less than 10 minutes if you have an injection called **syntometrine.** This can be given in your leg immediately after the baby is born. If the placenta is delivered naturally it could take up to an hour.

Phew! It's all over – time to start getting to know your new baby!

Different types of birth

NORMAL DELIVERY
Your baby comes down the birth canal and is delivered through your vagina.

Sometimes you may **need** some extra help to deliver your baby. Although things may have started off well you can become very tired and the baby can become distressed. So what sort of things are available to help deliver your baby safely?

VENTOUSE
(suction cap)
A suction cap/pad is used to help the baby out. It fits over the baby's head. Your baby's head may have some swelling but this will go down in a few days.

FORCEPS
Sometimes used for the same reasons as above. However, you may need to have an episiotomy.
So what's an episiotomy?

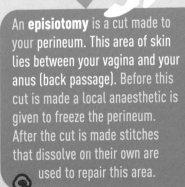

midwife

CAESAREAN SECTION
An operation to gently remove the baby from your womb. Some women may need to have a section because the baby is lying in an awkward position or because a medical problem has arisen. There are several main reasons for a planned (elective) section, which are:

- Low lying placenta
- Large baby
- Breech or any other awkward position
- Raised blood pressure
- Women who have had a previous caesarean
- Women who are expecting twins

You will know well before your due date if you are having a planned section and so will be prepared. However, sometimes you might have to have an emergency section because:

- The baby is distressed
- Failed inductions
- Failure to progress

An **episiotomy** is a cut made to your perineum. This area of skin lies between your vagina and your anus (back passage). Before this cut is made a local anaesthetic is given to freeze the perineum. After the cut is made stitches that dissolve on their own are used to repair this area.

dionne

There are some basic routine procedures that are followed:

- Before you go in you will have the operation discussed with you. You will need to sign a consent form.
- The top part of your pubic area will be shaved at the bikini line level. This area is where the surgeon will cut.
- You may have some medicine to settle your stomach.
- You will have a drip put into your arm.
- You will be offered a spinal anaesthetic (where you do not go to sleep) but your lower abdomen and legs will be numb.

The procedure

A small cut is made along the bikini line. Dissolvable stitches are used inside and removable ones are used on the top where your skin is stitched.

The whole operation can take up to an hour. Your hospital stay will range between 3 and 5 days.

You will have a catheter (tube into your bladder) at first, and a drip. You will also be given strong painkillers.

Will I be able to try for a normal delivery once I've had a section if I fall pregnant again?

Many women go on to deliver naturally the second time around. It will depend on how your next pregnancy goes and the reason for your first caesarean. You can discuss this with your obstetrician (lead doctor in charge of your care).

Recovery

You will need to give your stitches a chance to heal and may have to take painkillers for a few days. Your midwife will tell you about what you can and can't do in the first few days, but it can take 6–8 weeks to make a full recovery.

Pain Relief

It's really important you know what sort of analgesia (posh name for pain relief) is available, preferably before you arrive in the labour ward!

DRUG-FREE PAIN RELIEF (analgesia)

Ease the pain without taking any drugs.

ENDORPHINS

The body's own natural painkillers.

☞ Your brain is very clever and during labour will automatically release endorphins to help with the pain. Try and relax and go with the flow of your labour.

It's important to remember that **during your labour you may** change your mind about pain relief.

midwife

☞ Nature is kind in that after each contraction peaks you will have a recovery period. Deep breathing keeps your womb supplied with oxygen so your contractions work better. Think of contractions as positive pains, i.e. they bring you nearer to meeting your baby (OK, so it may not feel like it at the time, but it will all be worth it!).

WATER

Great for relaxing and relieving backache.

☞ You can take a warm bath or shower.

POSITIONS

Different delivery positions can make a difference to your labour.

🔹 Gravity helps the descent of the baby and helps the cervix to open, so try to remain upright as much as possible and hopefully it will all be over quicker. Standing upright also helps to increase the size of your pelvis.

🔹 Different positions you might want to try include: walking, squatting, kneeling on all fours, leaning on a wall or leaning on your birth partner.

TENS MACHINE

Trans electrical nerve stimulation.

🔹 Works by blocking pain and allowing your body to produce its own endorphins. Minute electrical impulses are sent through pads on your back.

MASSAGE

Massage is helpful to ease backache. This is where a birthing partner, like me, can make themselves really useful by massaging where necessary. Try using olive or vegetable oil to ease the strokes. If you want to try some aromatherapy-based oils speak to your midwife.

louise's boyfriend john

Advantages: You can control the amount of impulses sent, you can walk around with it and it can be hired late in your pregnancy for use at home.

Disadvantages: You will need help to put the pads on, and you can't use it in water. It's most useful when you first go into labour, but may help less after that.

Those are all drug-free pain relief options – but you could of course try having your baby with the help of drugs. **Read on for more options.**

DRUG-BASED ANALGESIA

I want whatever pain relief is available!

ENTONOX

Also known as laughing gas **(gas and air)**, used to take the edge off the pain.

You must be joking!

- You breathe it in through a mouthpiece only when you have a contraction.

- **Advantages:** It can be used with other forms of pain relief. You are in control of how much you take. The gas does not stay in your body and the oxygen is good for your baby.

- **Disadvantages:** It can make you feel sick, giggly or high. It can cause you to have a dry mouth so drink plenty of water and apply lip balm to your lips. Entonox will only take the edge off your pain; unfortunately it won't get rid of it altogether.

INJECTIONS

Injections of pethidene and diamorphine relax your muscles. These will make you relaxed and a little drowsy.

One of the advantages of injections is that they are very strong painkillers that will ease the pain. when I had my little boy.

dionne's friend Jane

- **Disadvantages:** Some women don't feel in control and cannot remember their labour. It can make the baby drowsy, which can affect the feeding and bonding processes after delivery. It needs to be given with an anti-sickness drug.

EPIDURAL

An anaesthetic which blocks the nerves to the lower back and legs.

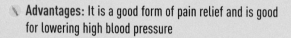

I asked my midwife about epidurals and she told me about some of the **advantages** and **disadvantages**

🖊 **Advantages:** It is a good form of pain relief and is good for lowering high blood pressure

🖊 **Disadvantages:** You cannot stand or walk and you have to rely on help to move. As you are monitored you will need a drip and possibly a catheter (a tube into your bladder).

Epidurals can slow down your labour. You may not be able to push very well due to reduced feeling, and this may lead to you having to have help with forceps or suction. It can be difficult to lie still when the epidural is being put into your back.

A few women may have a bad headache following the birth, but this will be monitored.

Life with the Baby

Baby M.O.T.

What happens once your baby is delivered?

Lots of checks and tests!

> **Wow!** It felt so **safe** and **warm** inside Mum's stomach. Suddenly I can hear all these **noises**, and see all these **lights** and **people**...

NEWBIRTH CHECK

So what about the tests and checks?

AS SOON AS THE BABY IS BORN the midwife will carry out a visual assessment of your baby's condition based on what she can see. This is called **Apgar scoring**. She will be looking at things like the baby's skin, e.g. if it looks pale or if it looks healthy. They will also check that the baby's breathing is regular and check its BODY TONE.

Physical examination at time of birth

Your baby will have a full physical examination. This will be carried out in front of you to check there is nothing wrong. The paediatrician (doctor for babies) normally does a more in-depth check before you are discharged from hospital, which includes checking the baby's reflexes, heart and lungs.

midwife

Once the baby is delivered they will need to be checked over by your midwife and will be handed back to you as soon as possible.

Skin-to-skin contact with your baby is really important, it will help them to feel safe and secure and get used to their new world.

Once the baby is **passed over to you, skin-to-skin contact** is really important to help you form a special bond. It also helps with breastfeeding.

Identification labels are put on the baby before you are moved to the ward and must be kept on during your hospital stay.

What exactly will skin-to-skin contact do?

- It will relax your baby as they already know your voice. Touch is a baby's first language and they can relate to soothing strokes.

- The baby will hear your familiar heartbeat, which will steady their own.

- Both of you will keep each other warm.

- This process starts the baby's first instincts of suckling and rooting.

Snuggle up and place your baby onto your bare chest. You could drape a blanket over both of you to keep warm if you need to. You could stroke and talk to your baby too.

Your baby's umbilical cord

louise's friend abi

My baby had a clip on to its belly button, which was removed by the midwife. The remaining cord dropped off naturally as it had no nerves in it.

The area left was cleaned with lukewarm water and then kept dry.

Vitamin K

Vitamin K is offered to your baby as either an injection or oral drops. It is needed to help the blood to clot.

You will be supported at home with visits from your community midwife.

Heel prick test

Also known as the 'Guthrie test', this is done within the first week of life to test for several conditions, e.g. sickle cell, a protein disorder called PKU and underactive thyroid gland.

Weight

After babies are weighed at birth, several days will pass before they are weighed again. We know that babies usually lose weight soon after birth for several reasons, one of which is the passing of meconium (their first poo!).

PREPARATION

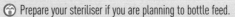

It is important to prepare for the first time you take your baby home. Here are some handy tips:

sarah's friend jess

- Prepare your steriliser if you are planning to bottle feed.
- Have a baby seat to transport your baby home.
- Make sure the house is warm enough for the baby.
- Try and get into a routine as soon as you can.
- Limit visitors at first so that you can rest. This might be difficult as everyone will want to see you and your newborn baby, but people will understand that they need to wait their turn.
- If you are expecting twins make sure that you have extra support.

Cot deaths (sudden infant deaths)

It is not yet known why some babies die suddenly for no apparent reason. To reduce the risk of cot death please use this guide, and also seek further help and advice from your health visitor:

- Place your baby on their back to sleep.
- Don't let your baby get too hot.
- Cut out smoking in pregnancy – fathers too!
- Do not let anyone smoke in the same room as your baby.

- Never fall asleep with your baby on a sofa or armchair.
- Keep your baby's head uncovered.
- Place your baby in the 'feet to foot' position (with their feet at the end of the cot or pram).
- Do not share a bed with your baby if you have been drinking alcohol, taken drugs or if you are a smoker.
- **The safest place for your baby to sleep is in a cot in a room with you for the first 6 months.**

The midwife will visit to check both you and your baby for a minimum of 10 days and a maximum of a month. She will not visit every day.

The health visitor will contact you around 14 days after your baby's birth. She will advise you on family health matters and the baby's development.

You can also receive additional support from your local Sure Start Children's Centre.

Who's going to be supporting and checking the health of you and your baby when you come home?

health visitor

midwife

TIREDNESS

- ✪ Rest when you can.
- ✪ Ask for help.
- ✪ Sleep when the baby sleeps if you can.
- ✪ Get support from friends and relatives.

dionne

EMOTIONS

Having a baby is a very emotional time. Baby blues can occur around days 4 to 6. You may become tearful but this will soon pass. Postnatal depression usually occurs in the first 8 weeks after the birth, though it can occur up to a year after the baby is born. You may not be back to your usual self for a while. Signs include:

- 🍼 Not being able to sleep
- 🍼 Lack of appetite and weight loss OR overeating
- 🍼 No interest in doing things
- 🍼 Not bonding with the baby
- 🍼 Feelings of hopelessness and guilt
- 🍼 Anxiety
- 🍼 Tearfulness

You may **feel happy at first** and relieved that your baby has arrived safely. However, **you may begin to feel worried about several things,** e.g. whether you are doing things correctly. **Don't worry,** it is only natural to feel like this as being a mother is a new experience.

If you think you have any of these symptoms speak to your health visitor. You shouldn't be ashamed – depression can affect 1 in 10 women but help is available. Don't hide the way you are feeling.

Sleeping
Babies can sleep more in the early weeks, waking often for feeds. As they get older they become more alert and are awake for longer periods.

Crying
Babies cry to communicate. However, some babies can cry constantly. Check with your GP to rule out any medical problems.

Checks
Check whether the baby is hungry and needs feeding

Soothing techniques
Gentle rocking
Dim lights
Soft gentle music
Baby massage
Motion, e.g. a car journey

Bathing
You can top and tail (wash face and bottom, but with a separate cloth or cotton wool) if you don't want to bathe daily.

Fit bathing into a routine, e.g. before bed time.

1 Days 1–2 Meconium

2 Days 3–4 Green

3 Days 5–6 Yellow

4 Day 7+ Larger

Urates or brick dust

False period Harmless light bleed

Nappy contents
Don't be alarmed if your baby has passed the following in their nappies:

😨 False period – a light spot/bleed from some baby girls.

😨 Pink/orange crystals which are salts in your baby's wee. It may be a sign that your baby needs to feed more often. Seek advice from your midwife.

Nappy change
The first poo is the black sticky meconium which then changes to a seedy yellowy green. **Breastfed babies** have a watery loose yellow frequent poo to start with. Bottle-fed babies pass medium firm yellow poos. Use barrier creams on your baby's skin.

Talk to your baby
Babies naturally respond to our voices, especially if we alter the tone or rhythm – i.e. 'cooing'.

CONTRACEPTION

Life with the Baby

Having sex may be the last thing on your mind; then again it may not! It's essential you use some form of contraception if you don't want another baby straight away. Your hormone levels are still high after giving birth and you could easily fall pregnant again.

Condoms are a good choice as they also protect from STIs. This is especially important when you start a relationship with a new partner.

It is really important that you find out about your contraceptive options and think about what will best suit you and your lifestyle.

Choices You can talk to your midwife, GP or health visitor to find out more about your contraceptive choices. Or you could visit a family planning clinic or one of the many young people's sexual health drop-ins in your area. **See page 76 for more information.**

Emergency contraception Accidents do happen, e.g. your condom may split or you may have unprotected sex (using no contraception). If this does happen you can use **emergency contraception. You have 2 options:**

Emergency hormonal contraception (EHC). This used to be called the morning-after pill. In fact you can take the emergency contraceptive pill up to 3 days (72 hours) after having sex. It's a single pill that can help prevent pregnancy.

An intrauterine device (coil). This can be fitted up to 5 days after having sex.

Whichever you use it's important to get help as soon as you can, as emergency contraception is more effective the sooner you take it. You can get help from your family planning clinic, GP and most chemists.

Relationships Having a new baby may put a strain on your relationship. Some partners will naturally understand that you must tend to the needs of your baby first. However, some partners will be resentful that most of your time is taken up with the baby. It is important that you keep communication channels open and talk to each other. You should only start having sex again when you are physically and mentally ready for it, not because you feel you have to.

Word search

Complete the word search to find out about the different methods of contraception available.

You need to find 6 methods of contraception. Here are some clues to help you:

1. This method comes in a packet and you normally take it every day. You may not be able to use it if you are breastfeeding.

2. This is easy to use, you stick it onto your skin and change it regularly. Cannot be used while breastfeeding.

3. This comes as a male and female type of contraception. It's also the only method that will protect you from sexually transmitted infections and is safe to use if you are breastfeeding.

4. This is a small plastic tube that fits under the skin in your arm. It can be used from 6 weeks after giving birth, even if you are breastfeeding.

5. These are generally T-shaped and fitted into the womb. Can be used even if you are breastfeeding.

6. This will be injected into your arm and lasts between 8 and 12 weeks. You can start using it 6 weeks after the birth, even if you are breastfeeding.

o	c	j	d	n	t	r	c	w	q
l	k	o	h	i	b	w	a	o	i
n	b	v	n	w	y	o	c	a	m
r	o	o	h	d	f	e	p	z	p
p	c	h	x	a	o	a	c	a	l
y	o	a	t	p	t	m	p	n	a
o	i	n	j	e	c	t	i	o	n
l	l	a	h	a	e	v	l	j	t
b	e	p	q	y	u	k	l	s	j
j	w	p	a	t	c	h	n	p	l

Find the answers to the clues on page 79.

68

Benefits

The following section is for under 18s and is intended as a guide only. You will need to speak to a specialist adviser to find out exactly what you are entitled to. In some cases these benefits will also apply to over 18s.

Universal Credit

A new single payment for people who are looking for work or on a low income, including new parents.

From October 2013, Universal Credit aims to bring together a range of working-age benefits into a single streamlined payment. This single monthly payment will replace parts of the old benefits system, replacing the following allowances and credits where a family or person qualifies:

- Income-based Jobseeker's Allowance
- Income-related Employment and Support Allowance
- Income Support
- Child Tax Credits
- Working Tax Credits
- Housing Benefit

How is a Universal Credit payment calculated?

Universal Credit payments depend on your circumstances regarding:

- Your children
- Childcare
- Carers
- Capability for work
- Housing

A Universal Credit payment covers everyone in a family who qualifies for support. This may be:

- A person claiming for themselves alone
- A person claiming for themselves and their children
- A couple making a joint claim for themselves
- A couple making a joint claim for themselves and their child or children

DO I GET UNIVERSAL CREDIT IF I AM 16–17 OR A STUDENT?

You can get Universal Credit if you are aged 16 or 17 if you have dependent children, or are pregnant between 11 weeks before and 15 weeks after the expected date of the birth of your baby.

Students do not normally qualify for Universal Credit. But you will be able to claim as a student if you have dependent children.

Contribution-based Jobseeker's Allowance

You can get this for up to 6 months if you have been working and have paid enough National Insurance contributions within the last couple of years.

This is a separate allowance from your Universal Credit.

jobcentre adviser

Most people will apply online. If you do not have a computer or do not know how to use one, there is help with your application either by telephone or at your Jobcentre Plus.

Universal Credit is paid directly into a claimant's bank account once a month.

For information on how to claim Universal Credit go to www.dwp.gov.uk or call Jobcentre Plus on 0845 6060 234.

What's what? Benefits insight

sarah's friend jess

There are many different benefits available to help you through your pregnancy, and further help is available once you've had your baby.

There are some benefits that everyone can get, which include:

- **Child Benefit** – most people get this once their baby is born. Ask at your local Jobcentre Plus or local Children's Centre.
- There are **free prescriptions** and dental treatment for people who are:
  - Under 16
  - Getting income-based Universal Credit
  - Pregnant
  - New mums who had a baby in the last year

Healthy Start provides you with free vitamins (C, D and folic acid). You will also get vouchers to buy fruit, veg, cow's milk (for you to drink) or infant formula milk from participating shops/supermarkets. Each voucher is worth £3.10 per week. Call Healthy Start on 0845 607 6823 or visit www.healthystart.nhs.uk. Ask your midwife or Sure Start Children's Centre for an application form and where to get vitamins.

Maternity rights

If you're working you'll have a variety of entitlements, such as:

- Maternity leave from work without losing your job
- Statutory maternity pay from your employer or Maternity Allowance
- Protection from unfair treatment and protection from being sacked because you're pregnant
- Child Benefit

For extra support and help with your maternity rights, speak to:

- Your union
- Your employer (or the personnel department if it's a large organisation/company)
- Jobcentre Plus
- Connexions
- Citizens Advice Bureau
- Sure Start Children's Centre

CHILD BENEFIT

Every couple where both parents earn less than £60,000 per year gets Child Benefit for each child they are responsible for (or a single parent earning less than this). You get a higher rate for your first child. Your parents can get child benefit for you if you're under 16.

Benefits

For more information contact
The Citizens Advice Bureau
www.adviceguide.org.uk
Department for Work and Pensions
www.dwp.gov.uk
Or visit your local neighbourhood office.
You may need to book an appointment.

COUNCIL TAX SUPPORT

You don't have to pay council tax until you are 18. After that, your local authority in England, or the Scottish and Welsh governments if you live in either of these countries, have their own systems of council tax support.

If you are on a low income you will get a discount on your council tax.

MATERNITY PAY

You could be entitled to some sort of maternity pay if you are working – either Statutory Maternity Pay (SMP) or Maternity Allowance (MA).

SMP STATUTORY MATERNITY PAY

Your employer pays this while you are on maternity leave, in the same way your wages would normally be paid. Your employer is repaid this money by the government. You should tell your employer that you intend to take maternity leave as far in advance as you can, so they have time to arrange for it to be paid.

MA MATERNITY ALLOWANCE

You can claim this using Form MA1 from your local Jobcentre Plus. You'll have to provide some information including proof of earnings. If you don't have wage slips you'll need a letter from your employer confirming your earnings. If you're still employed your employer will need to explain why you are not being paid SMP.

SURE START MATERNITY AND SOCIAL FUND GRANTS

If you are eligible to claim these grants the payments will be made as part of your Universal Credit.

You can apply for a £500 Sure Start Maternity grant any time after 29 weeks of your pregnancy and up to 3 months after your baby is born. Speak to your Jobcentre Plus for details on how to claim.

If you're under 16, your parents can usually claim it for you if they receive Universal Credits.

There may be some extra social fund loans and grants available, depending on your circumstances. Again, your parents may be able to claim for you if you are living at home.

You may also be able to get a Community Care Grant if you are moving into your own accommodation, to help you to buy things like a fridge, bed, cooker, etc. **Apply through Jobcentre Plus.**

CARE TO LEARN

This is funding available to help with childcare and travel costs whilst you continue in education or training, providing you are under 20 when you return to college. After you've had your baby Care to Learn will pay up to £160 per week (including during school holidays) to help you continue with your studies.

For information contact the **Care to Learn** hotline on 0800 121 8989 or visit www.gov.uk/care-to-learn

Child Support Agency

Even if you are not married to or living with **your baby's father, he still has to support his child financially.**

A Connexions PA is your own Personal Adviser at your Connexions office

The Child Support Agency (CSA) can arrange this and will work out how much money he'll need to pay to support his child.

The CSA can draw up an agreement about how much the father will pay if you cannot agree this between yourselves. Sometimes circumstances can change and you and your partner may separate so it might be best to get a proper agreement drawn up through the CSA in case this does happen.

The CSA has a really useful website www.cmoptions.org or you could speak to your Connexions PA, children's centre worker, health visitor or Jobcentre for advice about contacting the CSA.

*Benefits information correct at time of publication

Support, Advice and Options

Once you've had your baby

Registering the birth

You must register the birth of your baby within 42 days of the birth. You'll need to do this at the registry office and may need to make an appointment before you go.

As the father of your baby, if you are not married to the baby's mother and want to have parental responsibility (PR) you need to go with your partner to register the birth to ensure your name is on the birth certificate.

If you don't have PR you will not be able to make decisions about your child's life. It is possible to get PR after the birth has been registered but it involves filling in forms and may cost money.

See www.fnf.org.uk for information on father's rights

louise's boyfriend john

Where you will live and financial support

If you can stay at home in your own room and you feel happy there this may be the best option. You'll also get support from whoever you live with.

Where you live once you've had your baby is important. Living on your own in your own place might sound great but it's not easy.

You might end up somewhere quite grotty or a long way from your family and friends.

dionne

It also depends on your age as not many young people under 18 can get a tenancy agreement, so are less likely to be able to live independently as the council and most landlords are unlikely to give you an agreement.

This isn't always possible though, and it can be difficult for anyone with a new baby, particularly if where you live is not very big. You may also find everyone else is trying to take over when you just want to be Mum!

There are several options for housing but most people join the Housing Register to apply for a council property.

Anyone can apply to go on the Housing Register as long as they fulfil certain criteria. The register works on a 'banding' system. Applicants are placed in one of five bands based on their need for council accommodation. The bands run from A to E with people placed in Band A being in the greatest need for housing.

If you want to apply to be put on the Housing Register, **contact your local council and they will put you in touch with the relevant department.**

It is best to contact your council as soon as possible as applying for a property can take time and there may be a waiting list.

Returning to school, college, work or training

Pregnant/young Mum – under 16?

If you are still at school when you become pregnant or have your baby your Connexions Personal Adviser can help support you to stay on in school.

Depending on when your baby is due they can assist you to take any exams you are meant to be sitting or help you back into school once you've had your baby. You are entitled to the same maternity leave as any other dependant mum.

Pregnant/young Mum – 16 or over?

See pages 76–79 for contact telephone numbers

Some Connexions services have specialist workers to support expectant mums and young parents once you are 16. Normally they work with you until you're 20 but some people's circumstances may differ and they'll get continued support.

They can offer you support around many issues, particularly training, college courses and starting/returning to work.

For other help in getting a job you could visit a Jobcentre Plus, and if you are a single parent they have Lone Parent Advisers. Although anyone can go to the Jobcentre.

Local colleges and community centres offer a variety of courses from short 12-week tasters to full-time and degree level courses.

sarah

Services and Support

Health and Wellbeing

Start 4 Life and Change 4 Life

By introducing healthy habits right from birth, you can give your baby the building blocks for a healthy and happy future.

www.nhs.uk/Start4Life
www.nhs.uk/Change4Life

Frank

Information and advice about drug use.

0800 77 66 00
www.talktofrank.com

Young People's Sexual Health Clinics

There are sexual health clinics specifically for young people. Sexual health clinics operate across the county. Your own GP practice can also provide information about contraception.

You can find a local sexual health clinic through

www.brook.org.uk

And also through

www.nhs.uk/worthtalkingabout

Condom Distribution Scheme (CDS) (young people aged 19 and under)

For more information about free condoms telephone your NHS Primary Care Trust.

Domestic Violence

Freephone 24-hour National Domestic Violence Helpline

0808 2000 247

Healthy Eating During and Following Pregnancy

For more information and advice about healthy eating speak to your midwife or health visitor. You can also visit www.nhs.uk/livewell/healthy-eating or www.food.gov.uk

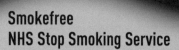

Smokefree
NHS Stop Smoking Service

The NHS Stop Smoking Service nurses and pregnancy support workers can give you, your friends and family extra help and support to quit smoking in a variety of settings to suit you.

Simply ask your midwife to be fast tracked into the NHS Stop Smoking Service or visit

smokefree.nhs.uk

Postnatal Depression

For more information about postnatal depression, visit the website

www.nhs.uk/conditions/postnataldepression

Family Support

Sure Start Children's Centre Services

Sure Start Children's Centre Services represent the bringing together of a range of services for children under 5 years and their families, including:

- Young parents groups
- Family support and parental outreach
- Support for children and parents with special needs

- Early years services
- Child and family health services
- Links with Jobcentre Plus (jobs, training and money)

Pregnant mums, parents and carers, including dads and male carers, are welcome to come along with their babies and children under 5 to join in with early learning, play and language activities, enjoy healthy snacks and meet friendly staff who can offer information and advice.

To find a Sure Start Children's Centre in your area visit

www.gov.uk/find-sure-start-childrens-centre

Family Lives

National organisation providing help and support in all aspects of family life

0808 800 2222
www.familylives.org.uk

77

Money and Employment

National Debtline

A national telephone helpline for people with debt problems. Offers expert advice over the phone and via email. The service is free, confidential and independent.

Helpline	0808 808 4000
Advice via the website	www.nationaldebtline.co.uk
Or email	advice@nationaldebtline.co.uk

Citizen's Advice Bureau

To find your nearest office visit — www.citizensadvice.org.uk

Connexions

A service offered to young people aged 13–19 years of age. Contact through Jobcentre Plus.

Jobcentre Plus

There are offices across the country, find out more on	0845 6060 234
Or contact information can be found online	www.gov.uk/contact-jobcentre-plus
Search for jobs on the website	www.gov.uk/jobsearch

Care to Learn

Provides an allowance towards childcare and travel costs for young parents 20 or under, who are either in or returning to education.

0800 121 8989
www.gov.uk/care-to-learn

Child Contact Information

National Association of Child Contact Centres

Promotes safe child contact within a national network of child contact centres. A child contact centre is a safe, neutral place where children of separated families can spend time with one or both parents and sometimes other family members.

Please call the information line for details of local centres	0845 4500 280
Or visit	www.naccc.org.uk

National Family Mediation

Mediation can help if you and your partner are struggling to talk about issues around your children.

You can call	0300 4000 636
Or visit	www.nfm.org.uk

Websites

National Childbirth Trust   www.nct.org.uk
Information for expecting and new mums and dads.

Just for Mums   www.justparents.co.uk
Tips and articles on parenting.

Net Mums   www.netmums.com
Local information for mums, including what's on, chat, parenting.

Twins and Multiple Births Association   www.tamba.org.uk
Provides information and support for families of twins, triplets and more.

Working Mums Jobs Website   www.workingmums.co.uk
Connecting mums with potential employers.

BBC Parenting   www.bbc.co.uk/parenting
Guide to pregnancy and birth and information for parents.

Worth Talking About   www.nhs.uk/worthtalkingabout
Information on relationships, sex and contraception for young people.

Citizen's Advice Bureau   www.adviceguide.org.uk
CAB website includes advice on benefits, debt, housing, etc.

Department for Work and Pensions   www.dwp.gov.uk
Benefits information.

Families Need Fathers   www.fnf.org.uk
Support keeping children and parents in contact.

Fathers Direct   www.fatherhoodinstitute.org
Information for young fathers.

Word Search Answers

1. Pill.   **2.** Patch.   **3.** Condom.   **4.** Implant.   **5.** Coil.   **6.** Injection.